Wonder-rig

Lee Duggan, Nigel Bird, David Annwn

KFS

Newton-le-Willows

Published in the United Kingdom in 2024
by The Knives Forks And Spoons Press,
51 Pipit Avenue,
Newton-le-Willows,
Merseyside,
WA12 9RG.

ISBN 978-1-916590-01-4

Copyright © Lee Duggan, Nigel Bird, David Annwn 2024.

The right of Lee Duggan, Nigel Bird & David Annwn to be identified as the authors of this work has been asserted by them in accordance with the Copyrights, Designs and Patents Act of 1988. All rights reserved. No part of this publication may be reproduced, stored in a retrieval system, transmitted in any form or by any means, electronic, photocopying, recording or otherwise, without prior permission of the publisher.

Illustrations by Nigel Bird:

1 of 4 Flock, p.3
2 of 4 Flock, p.9
3 of 4 Flock, p.15
4 of 4 Flock, p.23
Maquette Full, p.31
Reel, p.39
Rings, p.47
5 of 4 Faster, p.53
Circular Faster, p.61

Wonder-rig

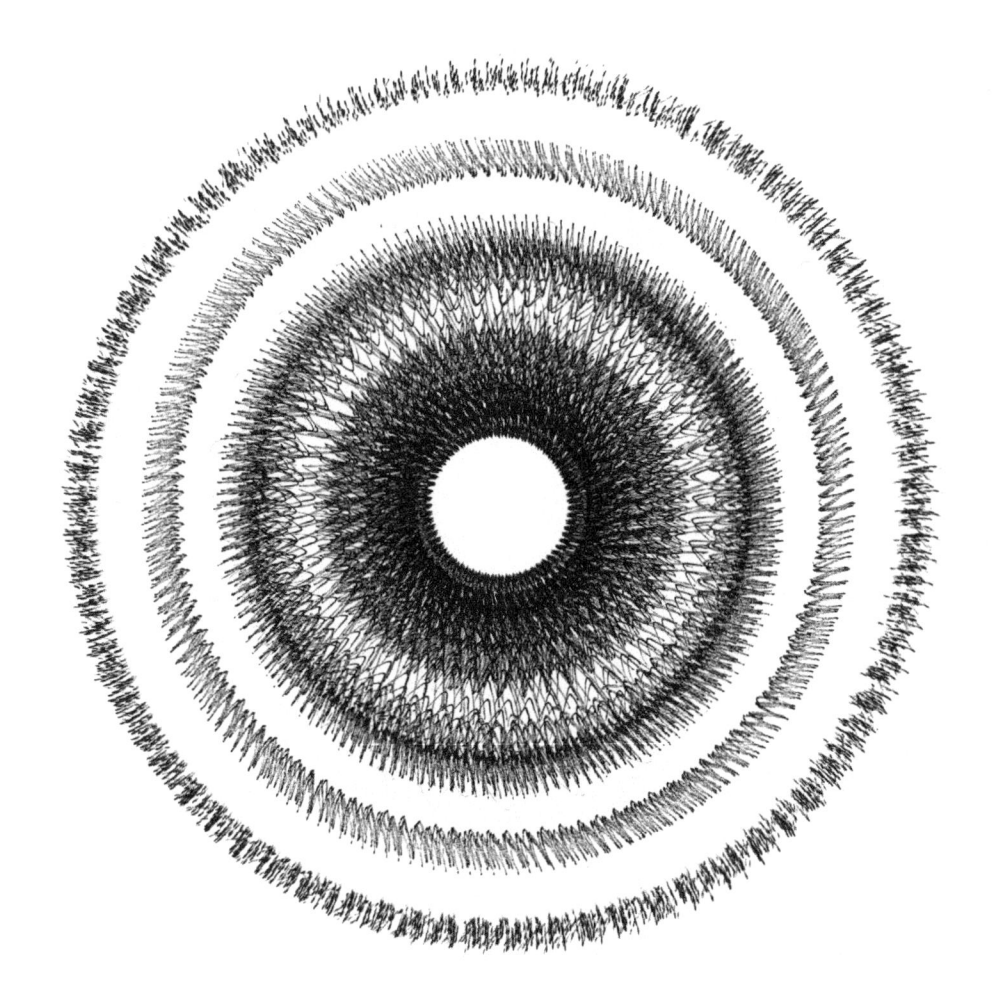

Lee Duggan, Nigel Bird, David Annwn

Marking-tracks

a decorative border

        marbled diamond
grey on brown – the way authority
transports in blazon

freezing tonight
see round wall at mid-
distance seems a couple kneeling
on paving, air flaring moisture
northern fleeting
mirage.
Sleet?

      a plastic strip called Roll & Stroll
lettering on the hand wash is illegible
as bar-code; the number-window
on the weighing-scales is blank

spaces between letters

Lee Duggan, Nigel Bird, David Annwn

then a man then crossing then road instant-
by-instant with large black
isosceles dog

snippets of attention
flicker, shaping round faces
then the deep haul.

An early morning dream
of palindromes
never odd or even

a small blue book in the school
library: the observers book
of heraldry

the sensuousness of colours
the sun with swirling rays
assembled beasts
hemmed into abstract fields

Wonder-rig

the way we read animals
; the ways
the squirrels in the maple over
John's Land-Rover perceive
magpies, crows
sharing trees (share?) terms
   we project: territorial,
my niche
claws against beaks

   our wormery:
a learn-
ed convocation forming
a ball of
roiled etymologies
and *eisenia foetida*
what are they passing
through skin to each other?
guesswork: give us
a clew Tigerworms

Lee Duggan, Nigel Bird, David Annwn

Perfume bottles slabs of glass
upside down house
reflection of itself
on margins, edge of

alien to earth the top layer is
rot, cascade of enzymes
where antennae of woodlice
flicker

gate-keeper to mycelia
and the architecture of
subterra

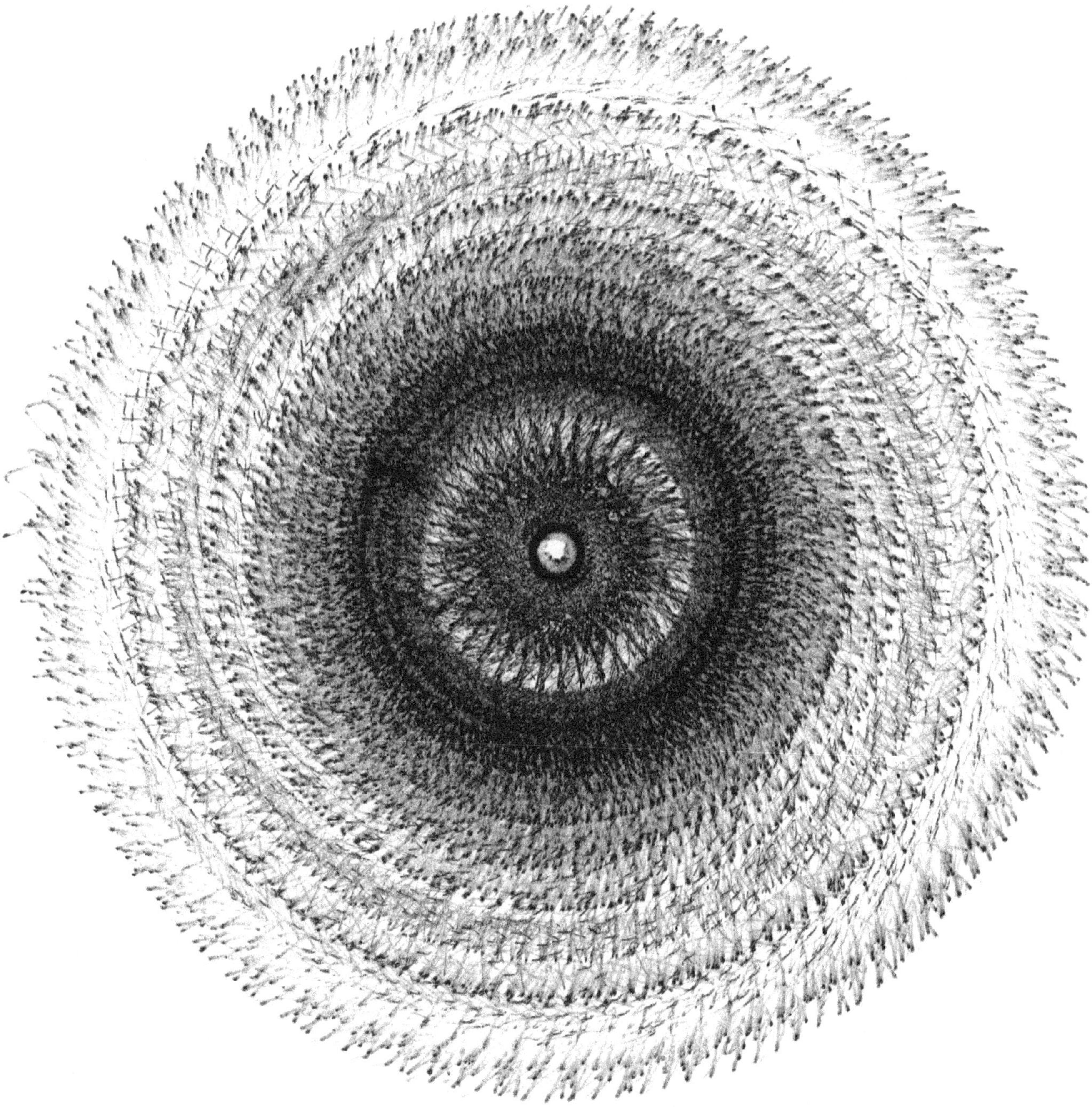

Wonder-rig

the last time I saw Lee
Harwood, Lee, was at Kelvin's
party at the Dark Barn
he was dressed as Tigger;

outside on the verge
a monument to an ambush
of the civil war

cats read height
as dominance: crow stands
sycamore top

inner domestic transposed
to outer: planners see signs, seats
bus-stops as 'street furniture'

dog pisses (scent-marks) wheely
what might the early hours freezing
fox make of this spray-
mosaic olfactory data-
scatter shining
pointilliste

illuminated hoardings

the ways we are wired
to pick out the face

this morning's the kettle's unreadable
reflection of this body,
a few light clouds –
a wake of dreams,
how we pass into day
behind us margins:
sleep's morass of
layered images

Wonder-rig

a priori proprioception
a habitation and a name-
scape we move
inside
breathing

wind moves round corner of the house
pressing windows blow, blow

climb from bed and see my things
there is a donkey with a robin on its back wearing
a turquoise bobble hat, a sheep with
a scarf, a collie and a duck
on the back in emboldened Gill Sans:
Medecins Sans Frontiers

Lee Duggan, Nigel Bird, David Annwn

Hello Hello
Looking up,
walking a street called Wood;
where sky starts
as the Welsh used to call it:
'traeth mundi'
oceanic space
marbled diamond

somewhere there are
habitable planets

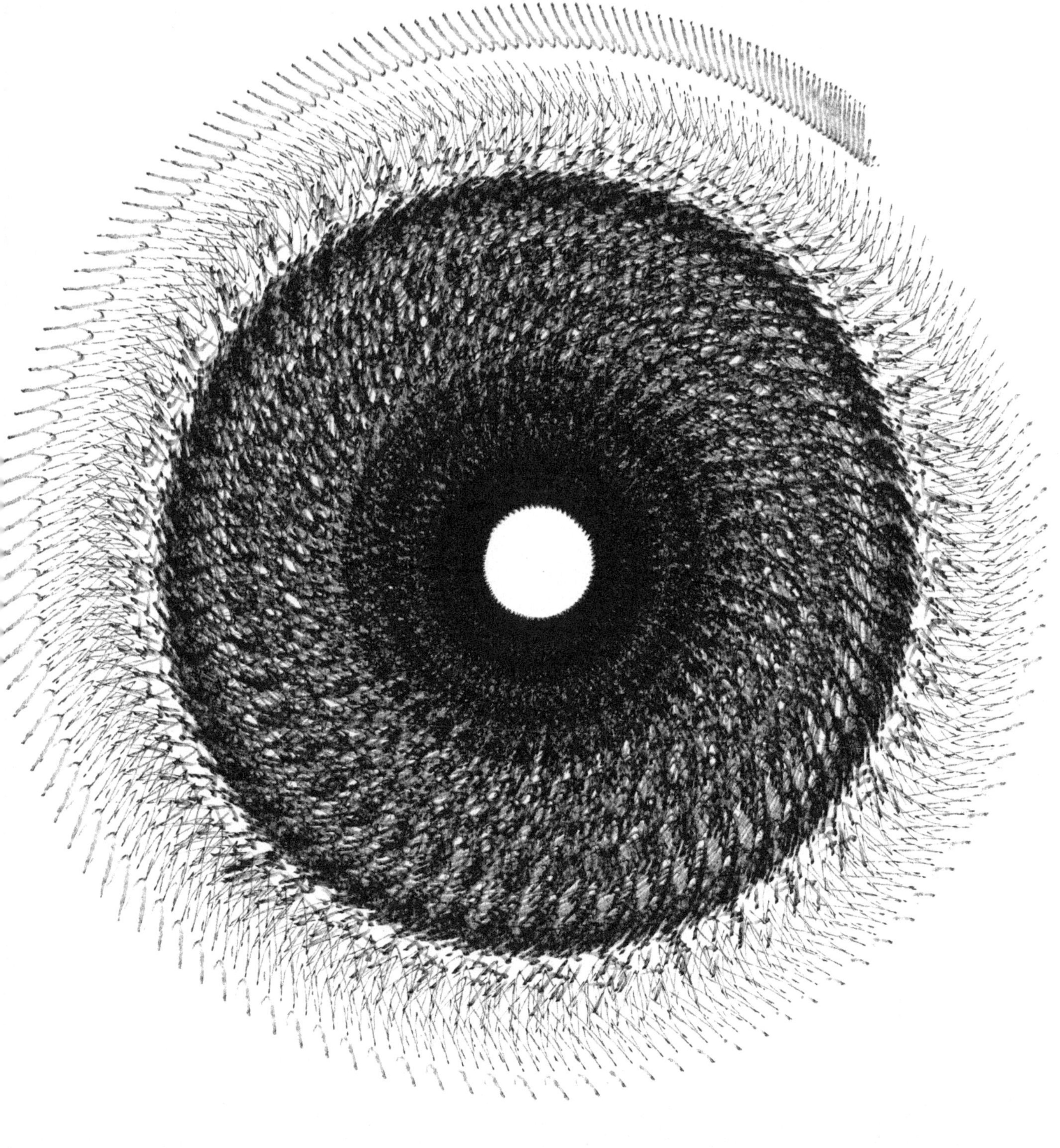

Wonder-rig

sometimes wander past a wine-bar
or pub and see the bartender looking
through glass
absently and wonder if she or he
is wondering what is that
other person out there thinking

first-floor vista
lightest snowflakes
hardly formed
softest dashes

Lee Duggan, Nigel Bird, David Annwn

bellow below
        field where fairies
                curse for each corner an element

   cauldron or ynys
   otherworld song
     to wonder
        some time
           the way we
   claw//
      one in
        front of
the-other

Wonder-rig

                               read //
                                            I
              // in animal
                    // the I

       marking-tracks
             this
              snow   flake
                  plume blue pluen   snō flāk

   as the Welsh   /
                 call it up   /
                            /   ————— slipped
                                         —————-   fonts for colouring

   slumber-through-waking
              no dreaming just winds & fears
              patchwork stoning

Lee Duggan, Nigel Bird, David Annwn

breath of ritual gently warmed.   the last party.   wishing it   true
always to return   this runaway
  smelt lleawch   tone
laqua bright

                            —––-running home   to
from   river bed
howl at a house
empty as heaven
& no stars to hold
this bodily moment
free from system revolve

immortalinfinity
    curse this luminous drawing out
    natural presence in space
casting
  moss-clung-branches
 in reflection
    & bent enrippled
      Guises

        what does she do there deep & silent

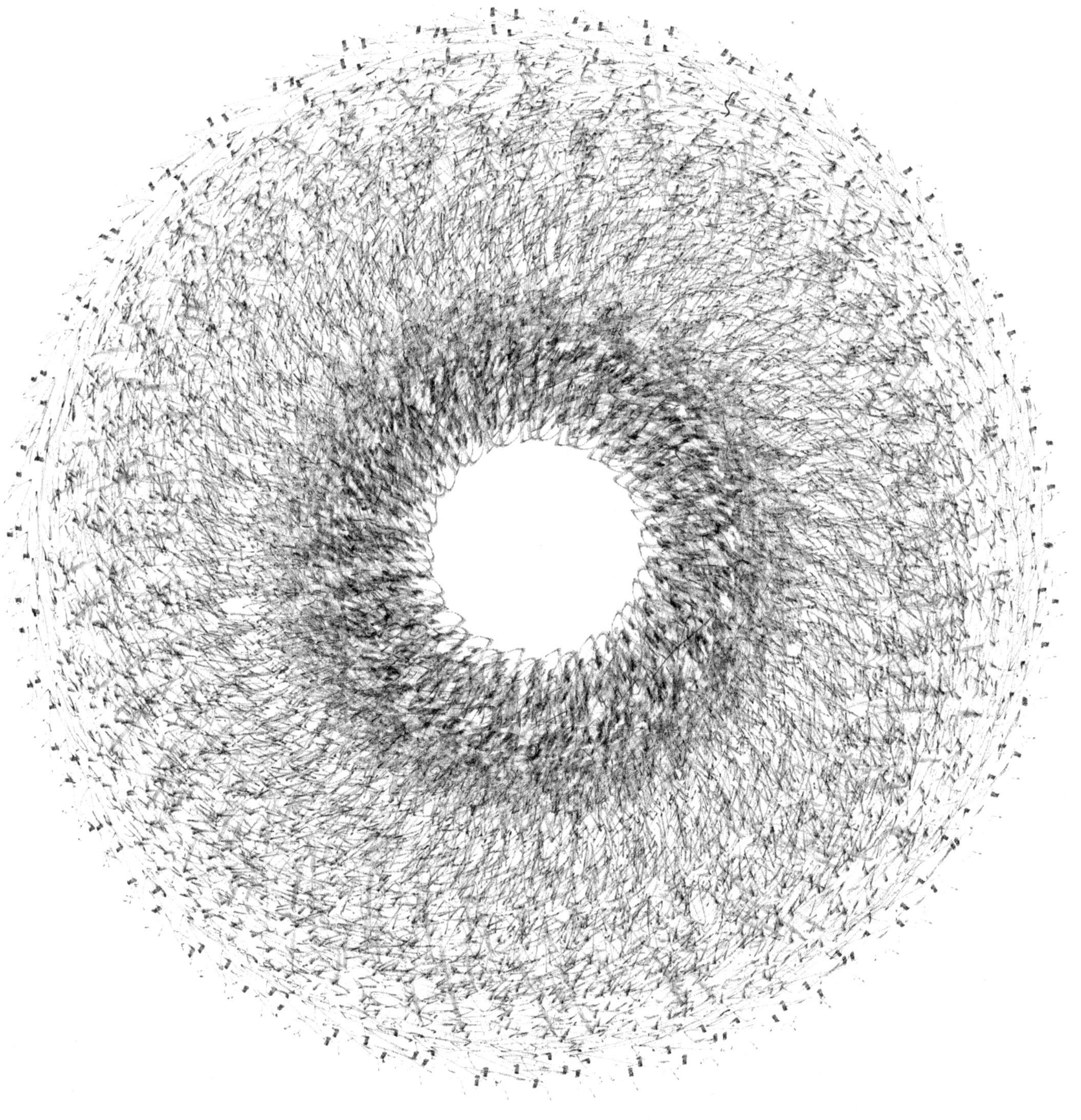

Wonder-rig

conceived through concave
tight as everything
      lets go
        for this
                masquerade is everywhere

where we left
      what were we thinking in
    stubborn spirals of
   refusal to unfurl
red crescent palms as the fists let go
let that left inside drift

Lee Duggan, Nigel Bird, David Annwn

                                                mist of me
                without trumpet or whirlwind
      when the day turns
     coffee shakes
  keys turn
another   day ticked off
               your donkey
                      in the background
always a robin as we dig
& worms slow in tarp tunnels
understand our suffering

Wonder-rig

nothing to say as   out of hand words   get in the way

case studies accompany the wrong shots
              an open road burning bridges
loving the edging   but next spring will reshape
            create off-centre-borders
      tree roots unruly with foundations
        measuring time as lines become me
go to jelly to the wolf & to the devil inside
lifted lyrics from the city despite all this green
   wonder of it all   as shop fronts blur   in sleeted revelry & early wanderings

branch-shadow on green-

thousand pale sails tucking in moss:
seed apostrophes shifting

Lee Duggan, Nigel Bird, David Annwn

                                          scarifying
                            striating gather handfuls

                 state masquerade: 'myrdd a myrdd garchara'

apse of sine
synapse last night's (raining off on)
confused and happy dream:

a houseful of poets and kids and partners coming in
    all fresh but somewhat chaotic, pleasure centres all touched off –
it always was
a teacher says 'I love you' / I hope he's not gone

putting plate next to plate a zen occupation

Wonder-rig

High contraries
buffeted attempts the gull fluctuates
on blue between two con-trails

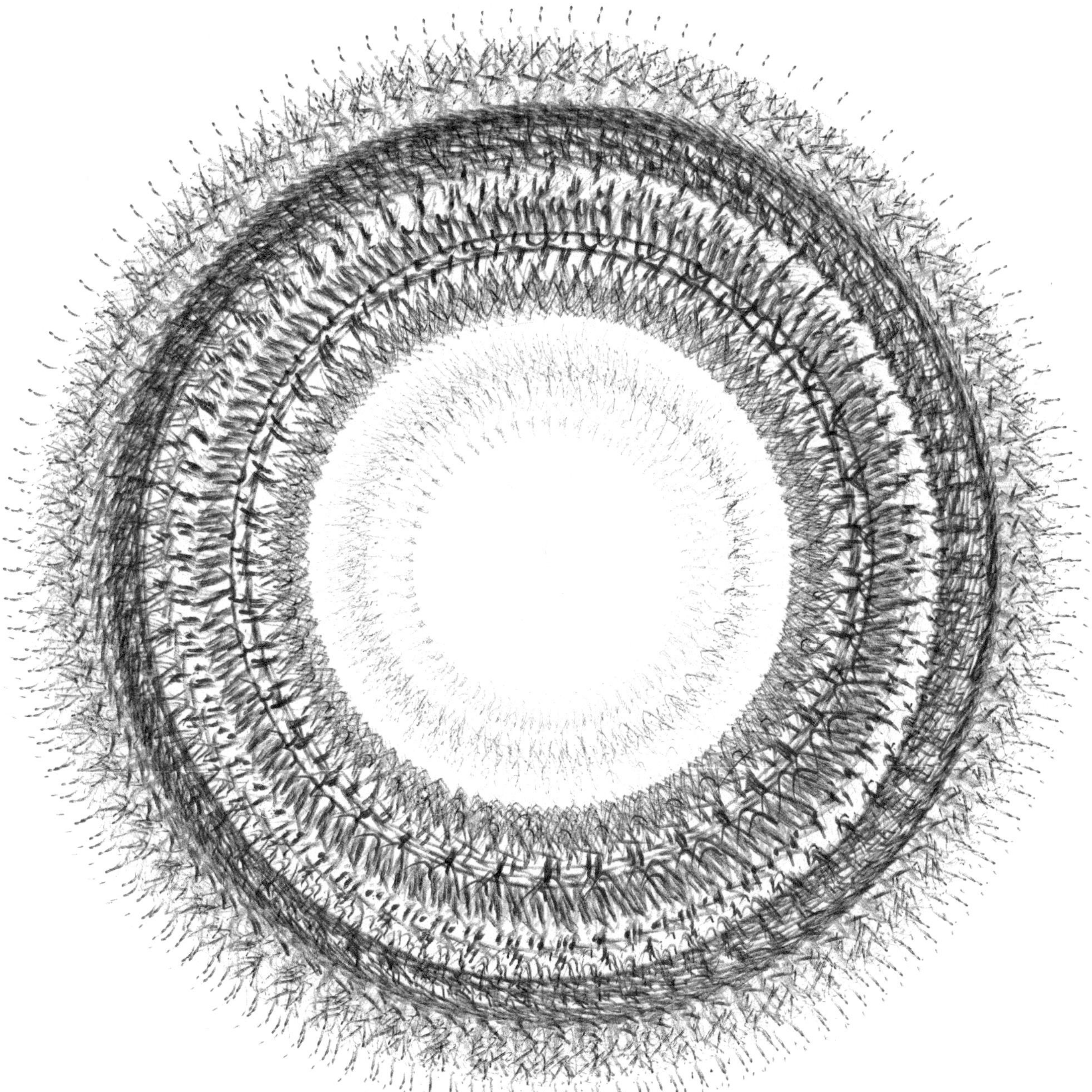

sibyl bisyllables:

Experiment 2, infants were significantly more likely to retain information about bisyllables that shared the same initial consonant-vowel syllable. Finally, the authors investigated—

—it says iPlayer
        go to pink-filled screen
                                            retina dilating
                          w/ photons despatched

filigrees

                finned phonemes
snowdrop: flurries; elixir helix
leaves folded back

Lee Duggan, Nigel Bird, David Annwn

graffiti city-peripheries
                              knock   cons

ciou   snes

                    ss

round: pinball   zinged by slingshot kicker

starting up to be fami-   liar, to honour that and give it time
in situ

                          bundled muscle runway sun
shadow strengthens in lowlight taking

Wonder-rig

singing dancing retail synched to lips

washer dryer's O / on TV Dusty works up
to big arms-candling
'Believe me!'
then lets it go with fingers fanned outwards once 57 years ago now
moon holds tree holds moon

Lee Duggan, Nigel Bird, David Annwn

```
                        evening   all   afternoon
                         turning  this   regalia
                        most  days  going  through
              vertical  rectangles   to   different   views
                bilateral:    sensed    and    continuous
              thought    joined    dot   –   to   –   dot
              i                              d    e    n    t
                i                                         ty
                  walking mammal  a  certain    height
```

Wonder-rig

in doorway closed Mark w/ crutches at his side & empty cup & shows his calf & foot
bruise mottling 'you talk you talk to me about
just
ice'

a treatise   owning a certain beginning, mid-dle
index going like print through rock,
and friends

abrades a braid
                          follicles and tendencies
                            top of the hour
                           Been a long time
                              Ring out
                               those
                               bells

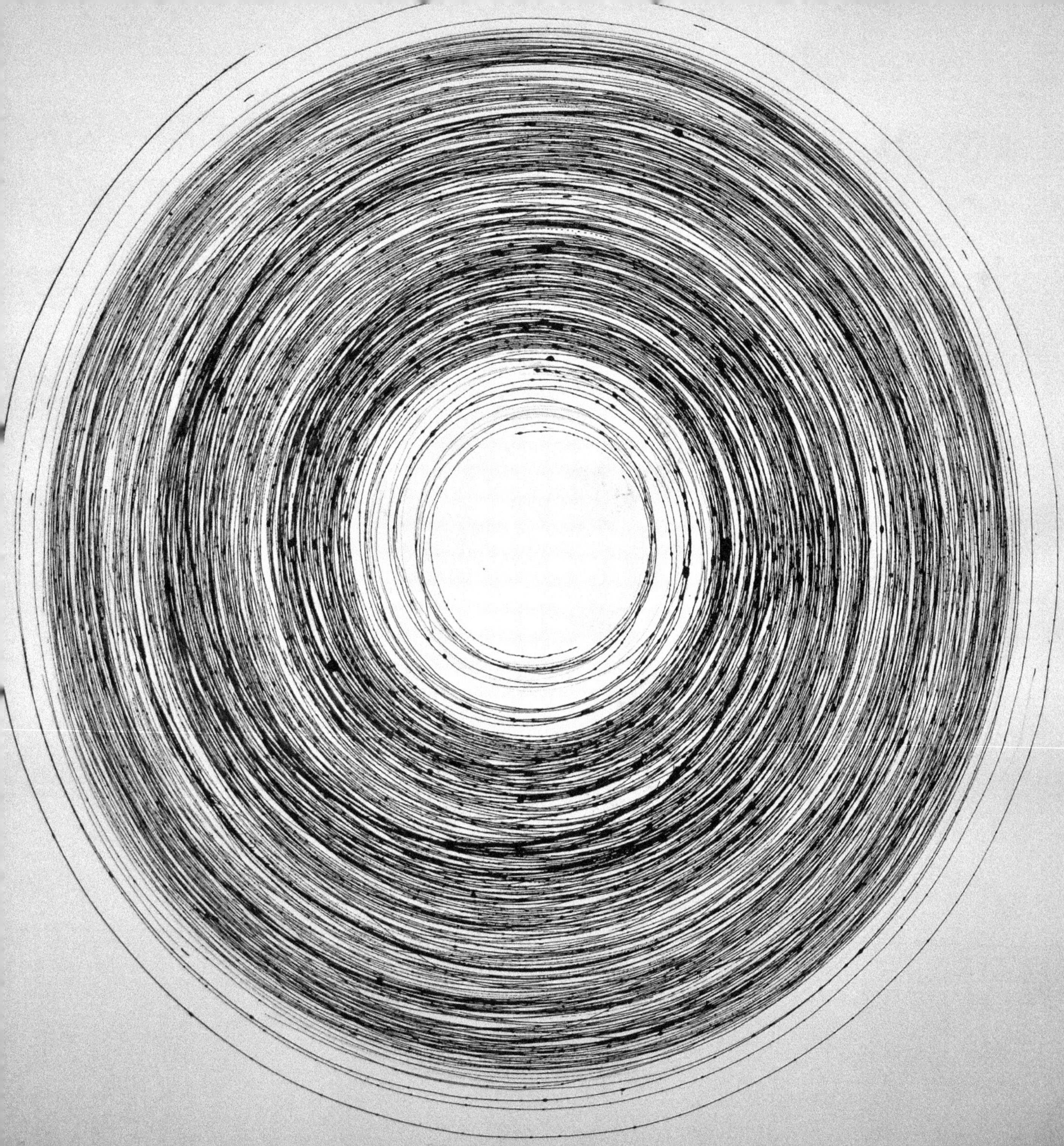

Wonder-rig

                        regalia

tone
laqua bright

            what does she do there deep & silent

conceived through concave
            rigmarole
rig of roles

Lee Duggan, Nigel Bird, David Annwn

lie here light
for waking, just a minute, dawning
　　　　　　　　i and **or** passing through each other
mirror, turning worlds fy ngair a gair fy mamau
testosterone rain

at the meetings of
intersecting worlds, sense-worlds
of insects and animals
radiating so differently in detail
waves antennae data
perceived spreading
enrippled
overlapping
chords and lenses

Wonder-rig

we won't be able to see the dark universe
but infer it from the movements of the visible

faintest wobbles in a star

'Between the sapphire and the sound
uncurls the rose of vision'

where do these guys go
spoor of water-dots on the side
of the cafetière

Lee Duggan, Nigel Bird, David Annwn

each morning, pills in hand
think pharma: the white cloaks
and tetrahedrons under the scanner
the crystals going round a local estate

so the mind drifts
                         what comprise

rejuvenate renew mayhap.
                      The color deep red is
Your lucky color. The hours between 4.30
and 5.30. are most auspicious

Wonder-rig

take winged word
back to hangar, strip to renew:

'Of good omen from Latin *auspicium*
'divination by observing the flight of birds
from auspex (genitive *auspicis*) + -<u>ous</u>

Lee Duggan, Nigel Bird, David Annwn

fix the NHS upstream – a deep affection
this TV tory twists her hands / torso:

'To live busy lives' repeating 'Look'
(we are looking)
That pay is a matter should people stay
/away hospital/ come forward / any sense

patient / when / at risk / the sooner
no you fucking don't / fewer people

treated/ demand / freud-slips her inner
lips saying 'emergency scare' instead of

'care': there you go as the fastfood deliverer
said to the tipless finger

Foreshadowing
shadow education minister
fluffing on-air:
'plucking a finger' (figure) 'out of the air'

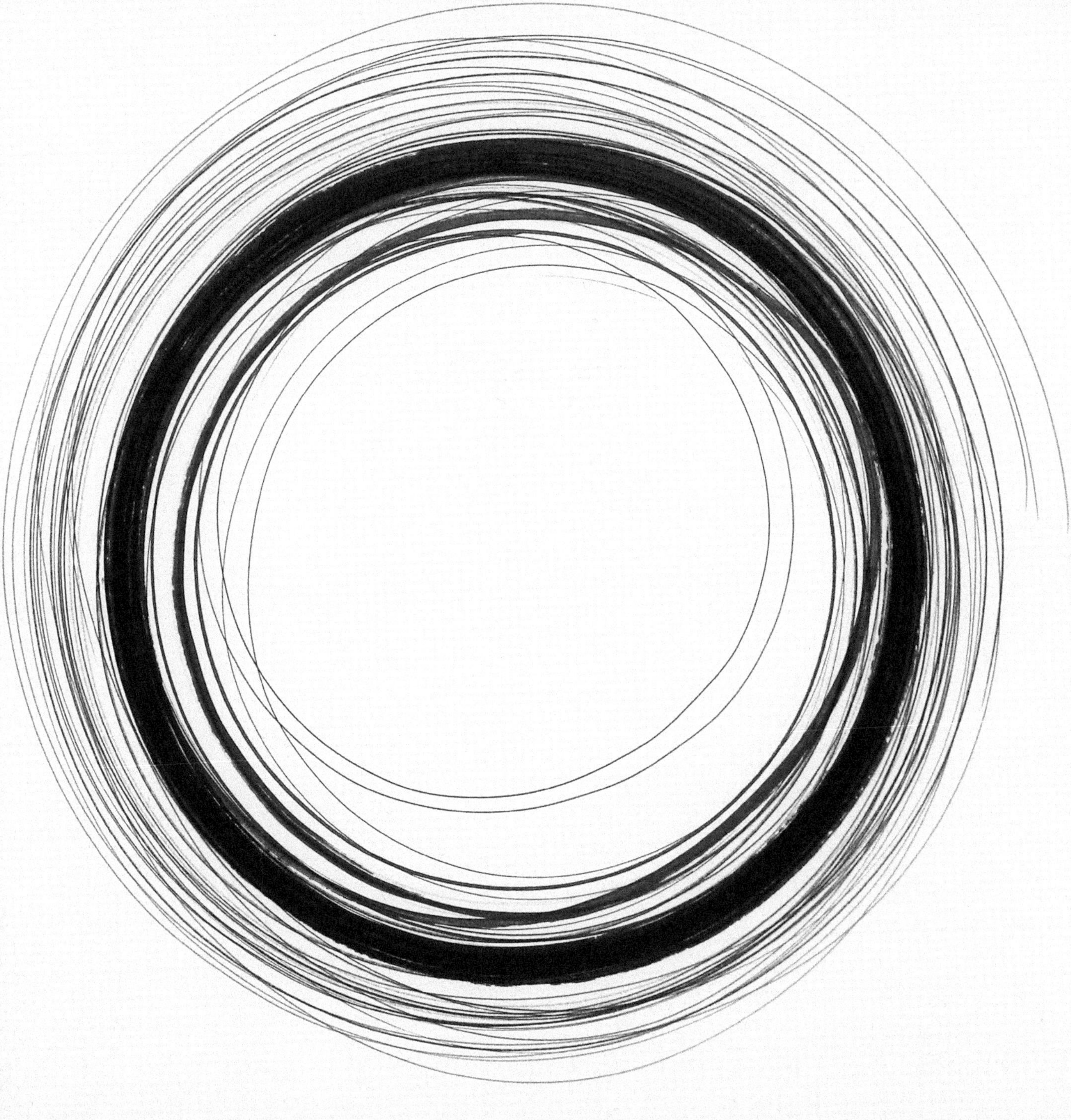

Welbeck is not well beck

375-hectares of 'new' City Fields
        development downhill as if to kiss
Aire and Calder water
                soil polluted with sheep carcasses
body parts,
                        biological waste:
piped off toxic methane
        will take three lifetimes to clear
in a park they say
        they'll build for children to play
'Public art will be integrated
into City Fields to enhance its environme — '
greenwashing & artwashing
Poems aren't a prophylactic
Sculptures by Mitcheson &
Broadbent: 'I was inspired to
create something —
recognisable images
of insects and wildlife
found at the side — '

Lee Duggan, Nigel Bird, David Annwn

how quick artists set off
on their 'natural trip' lyric
without the land –
or what they're being used to conceal
or thought of
micro-lives already
killed in the building

lucciola
fireflies
scintillas or cedillas of light
the human body
bioluminescent faintly

And all I've done for want of wit to memory
now I can't recall
by observing the flight of birds

your lines re-visit:
without trumpet or whirlwind
    when the day turns

Wonder-rig

on the wall
a cattle egret
between the orange flowers and white

at the side
volcanic soil
umber to umbra to black

sun
this morning
through my glass of water
puts down its message
for my eyes only
a twisting helix of light

Lee Duggan, Nigel Bird, David Annwn

changeling: letters, air, sand

silica crystal
will to see shapeliness
                           geomme-
tries
                               patterns
when we are threaded, zoned
and neuron-ed in, programmed
to read the system our minds
emerged from
intrinsic part of self-weaving
tapestry – is extrinsic
odd or
even there?

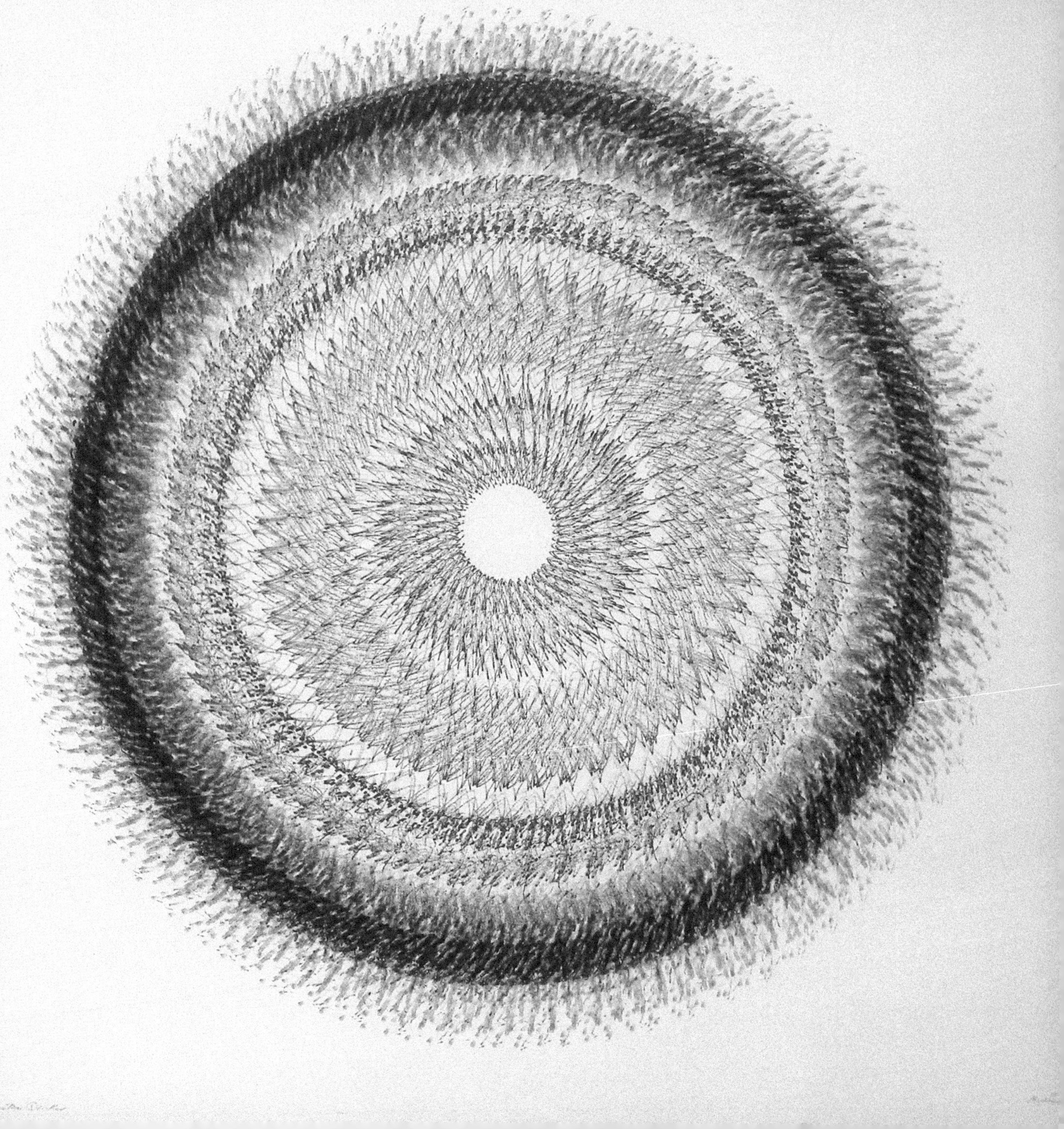

Wonder-rig

scoped
outside our visible range
teeming seethe chimeras
eaten and merging minutiae

        look down at us through tatters: freezing cumulus

by observing
        the flight of birds

                create off-centre-borders

plucking a finger out of the air

    when slips were what is needed/ to break through

the I

  marking-tracks

Lee Duggan, Nigel Bird, David Annwn

been off track n=more
    than is usual for
        the season/where words sunk
 dug through May abandoned
        above tree-line coppa
                found moon turn
    reed & kingfisher story
 tearless the rest of me ran to source
            tugging threads & thrashing

for what was more than
        dried bean-pods & bolting
     this oeuvre of the body
        leaving abstraction in my eyes & on the tip
     this tongue slowly
   turn in favour of avoidance
       dancing through to autumn
    earth burn & blight
      to nowhere

Lee Duggan, Nigel Bird, David Annwn

        drain to dregs out of this back yard
            bigger pictures in scripture & in stain glass
      mosaics & tapestries we praise
no news in this poem
        politics cut with trees
    the boys can't cry either/so we walk on one foot in
      broken ground feet to forest flooring us
     whisper ancient Yew & wait for a message in the well
drowning sailors broken into skies of stone
the possibility to fall through apart
                           & what is this

Wonder-rig

                  don't look to poets
              brooding on skyshapes
                    dreams of limbs smashed at the bay
& bits of lyric in the Gavi
     & somewhere else
          under Sportoletti
                right rib
              they say my pulse is slow & jolts
          purple at the lips & held together with string
    no pull or touch
               line it all with linseed in the porridge
danced off score
        left spinning
    we are all star dreaming
        to the end
              & what is this

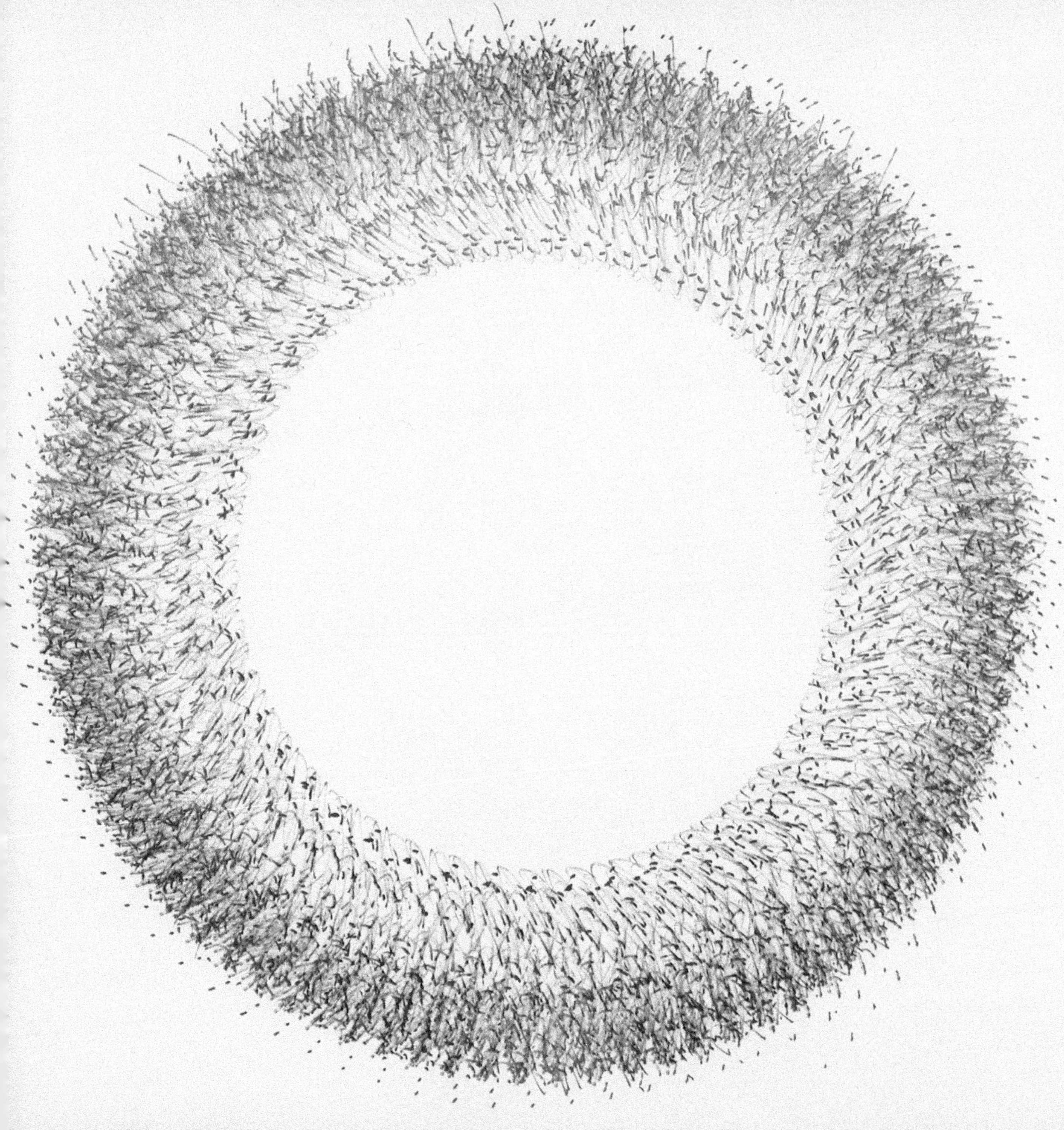

Wonder-rig

fly & draw breath
        to new birds
   read chai from the dead
          dealing possibilities
     jagged edges rearrange the heart
keep the pieces tidy & make room
      Luca papoosed so I don't drift off the edges
a brittle branch where my name hangs
        walk through river to mud
     a fat dipper splash
    takes me back to rain on moss on me
pick up & move on
         charcoaled white against grains of green
    suspended beat for a stolen
  concertina side view smiles
     haws line my pockets

Lee Duggan, Nigel Bird, David Annwn

a trumpet exclamation as I spin off the path
 into slower versions
 the sea once reached Llangefni
boom boom boom board against bittern
 kissing & kissing

Wonder-rig

new lines crease through me
    dried & cursed a
gypsy posey held in lace
    imaginary locks of hair & first smiles
      sweet as their last
        alone & open
    with precision place stones & shells
a clay bowl of green
      for new beginnings
  & what might be

Notes

Wonder-rig

In this sequence Lee Duggan writes 'this oeuvre of the body', foregrounding humans interacting with and reading the natural environment of which our perceptions are only an infinitesimally-small part. The poem's lines move variously in 'green / wonder of it all', shifting between perceptions and through wild and domestic life.

A rig can be a ridge, a strip of unplowed land, the centre of a piece of unmarked cloth, a dance, a song, a carriage and an arrangement. As a verb it can mean to prepare a ship's sails or to search. Each natural body is a complex array, a wonder rig.

There are different lexes at play and the Welsh language involved in: **'traeth mundi'** (p.14) – world strand; **'ynys'** (p.18) – island; **'pluen'** (p.19) – a feather; **'lleawch'** (p.20) – lie down; **'myrdd a myrdd garchara'** (p.28) – myriads and myriads of prisons; and **'fy ngair a gair fy mamau'** (p.42) – my word and my mother's word.

Duggan uses **'laqua'** (pp.20 & 41) as a water reference, Laqua means by the water or as a name in French a person living by the water, 'I have played with these words … in Italian it is l'acqua but this is directly the water and I didn't want that so keeping it as one word should work, I want a sense of colour and sheen too, acqua can refer to high water/tide peaks, it also has connotations to foot soldiers'.

Lee Duggan, Nigel Bird, David Annwn

Through innovative approaches and responses to the local environment Lee Duggan facilitates 'Walking with Words' workshops. Her debut collection, *Reference Points* (Aquifer 2017) received positive reviews in *Poetry Wales*, *Elliptical Movements*, and *Litter Magazine*, along with review of her sequence *Green* (Oystercatcher 2019). Her work appeared in the important anthology of contemporary Welsh innovative poetry, *The Edge of Necessary* (Aquifer & Boiled String, 2018). Recent collections include *Residential Poems* (Aquifer 2022) and *In Those Shoes* with Contraband Books, 2023.

Much of Nigel Bird's work originates from Landscape. His recent work is as much to do with the process of making as it is about what he sees, hear, smells, tastes, feels or touches. It is the nature and character of the place that inspires him; how it might have been made and its spiritual significance are features that inspire him to make his Art. His 'Flock' series of drawings are part of a collection of work inspired by sound: "During the time I lived in Southern France, I once had the good fortune to be walking underneath the formation of a flock of Starlings, which I believe is called Murmuration. The sound of their beating wings was quite deafening and I thought then that I needed to make a drawing about what I heard."

David Annwn is a land activist, his *turbulent/ / boundaries* (Westhouse 1999) revealing his and his group's fight to keep the last green fields in Wakefield, his *Resonance Fields* (Aquifer 2021) exploring his childhood in Cheshire sand quarries and *Wonder-rig*, the present sequence, showing readings of nature and confrontations with local government about one the biggest landfill site in Europe. Poems in his *Disco Occident* (2013) and *Redbank* (2018), both from Knives, Forks and Spoons, consider, respectively, the effects of tourism and war on landscapes. His book on eco-vampires of the silent screen has just been launched by Palgrave. There have been exhibitions of Thomas Ingmire's calligraphy of Annwn's poetry in Boston and San Francisco.